KLEIN HOLMES

700 Useless Facts to Make you Smart

First edition

This book was professionally typeset on Reedsy.
Find out more at reedsy.com

Contents

1

Space

Astronaut
Mars
Rings
Robot arms
The moon
Gravity
The sun
Jupiter
Moons
Earth
Uranus
Rocket
Mercury
Saturn
Space Suit
Neptune
Venus
Planets
Orbit
Asteroid
Space shuttle

Space is completely silent because there is no air for sound to travel through.

The Milky Way galaxy, where our solar system is located, is estimated to contain over 100 billion stars.

The sun makes up about 99.86% of the mass in our solar system.

The International Space Station (ISS) orbits Earth approximately every 90 minutes.

Astronauts on the ISS experience 16 sunrises and sunsets each day.

The largest volcano in the solar system is Olympus Mons on Mars, about three times taller than Mount Everest.

Space is not completely empty; it contains gas, dust, and particles.

The Hubble Space Telescope, launched in 1990, has taken some of the most incredible images of distant galaxies and nebulae.

There are more stars in the universe than there are grains of sand on all the beaches on Earth.

The concept of black holes was first proposed by physicist John Michell in 1783.

A black hole's gravitational pull is so strong that not even light can escape from it, making it invisible.

The speed of light is approximately 186,282 miles per second (299,792 kilometers per second).

The Andromeda Galaxy, our closest neighbor, is about 2.537 million light-years away from Earth.

The space between galaxies is expanding, causing the universe to grow larger over time.

One of the largest known structures in the universe is the Sloan Great Wall, a vast cosmic filament spanning hundreds of millions of light-years.

The famous "Pillars of Creation" in the Eagle Nebula are vast columns of gas and dust where new stars are being born.

Astronomers believe that around 96% of the universe is composed of mysterious dark matter and dark energy, which cannot be directly observed.

The temperature of outer space is just a few degrees above absolute zero (-459.67°F or -273.15°C).

There are more than 170 moons in our solar system, with Jupiter having the most at 79.

The largest moon in our solar system is Ganymede, which belongs to Jupiter and is even larger than the planet Mercury.

Pluto, formerly considered the ninth planet, is now classified as a "dwarf planet" since 2006.

The Great Red Spot on Jupiter is a massive storm that has been raging for at least 350 years.

Uranus and Neptune are known as "ice giants" because they contain large amounts of water, ammonia, and methane ice.

Saturn's rings are made up of countless small particles, ranging in size from a grain of sand to a house.

The first human-made object to reach space was the German V-2 rocket on October 3, 1942.

The first human to travel to space was Yuri Gagarin, a Soviet cosmonaut, on April 12, 1961.

The Apollo 11 mission, which landed humans on the moon for the first time, was launched on July 16, 1969.

The moon has no atmosphere, so it has extreme temperature fluctuations between day and night.

Astronauts on the moon experience only about 17% of Earth's gravity.

Space tourism is becoming a reality, with private companies planning to offer trips to space for civilians in the near future.

The "Big Bang" theory is the prevailing explanation for the origin of the universe, suggesting that it began as a singularity and expanded rapidly about 13.8 billion years ago.

The sun is about 4.6 billion years old and is roughly halfway through its life cycle.

Space is a near-perfect vacuum, meaning it has extremely low pressure and density.

The farthest human-made object from Earth is the Voyager 1 spacecraft, which left the solar system in 2012 and is now in interstellar space.

Spacewalking astronauts wear a special suit called an Extravehicular Mobility Unit (EMU) to survive in the vacuum of space.

The Kuiper Belt is a region beyond Neptune containing icy objects and dwarf planets, including Pluto.

The asteroid belt, located between Mars and Jupiter, contains millions of rocky objects, with Ceres being the largest known asteroid.

The first exoplanet (a planet outside our solar system) was discovered in 1992 orbiting a pulsar.

The heaviest known element in the universe is oganesson, with an atomic number of 118.

A day on Venus is longer than a year on Venus, taking about 243 Earth days to complete one rotation.

The largest known star is UY Scuti, with a diameter over 1,700 times that of the sun.

The first woman in space was Valentina Tereshkova from the Soviet Union, who flew in 1963.

The Voyager Golden Records, sent aboard the Voyager spacecraft, contain sounds and images representing life on Earth and are intended to be a message to potential extraterrestrial civilizations.

Space debris, such as old satellites and fragments from rocket launches, poses a risk to satellites and spacecraft in orbit.

Astronauts experience a reduction in bone density during prolonged stays in space due to the lack of gravity.

The largest known structure in the observable universe is the Hercules–Corona Borealis Great Wall, a filament of galaxies stretching over 10 billion light-years.

Space is not completely dark; there is a faint glow called the "cosmic microwave background radiation," which is leftover from the Big Bang.

The Great Attractor is a gravitational anomaly that influences the movement of galaxies in our local universe.

A day on Mercury is longer than its year, with one day lasting about 176 Earth days and one year lasting about 88 Earth days.

The James Webb Space Telescope (JWST), set to launch in the future, will be the most powerful space telescope ever built and will explore distant galaxies and stars.

2

Art & Literature

Vincent van Gogh only sold one painting during his lifetime.

The Mona Lisa has no visible eyebrows because it was fashionable in Renaissance Florence to shave them.

Shakespeare's plays and sonnets contain over 30,000 unique words.

"The Great Gatsby" by F. Scott Fitzgerald was initially considered a commercial failure.

Leonardo da Vinci could write with one hand and draw with the other simultaneously.

J.K. Rowling's "Harry Potter and the Philosopher's Stone" was rejected by 12 publishers before being accepted.

The world's largest library is the Library of Congress in Washington, D.C., with over 170 million items.

Pablo Picasso could draw before he could walk.

"Frankenstein" by Mary Shelley was written when she was just 18 years old.

The Bible is the best-selling book of all time, with over 5 billion copies sold.

The longest novel ever written is "In Search of Lost Time" by Marcel Proust, with over 1.2 million words.

The first known novel is "The Tale of Genji" by Murasaki Shikibu, written in Japan around 1000 AD.

The word "robotics" was introduced in a science fiction story by Isaac Asimov in 1941.

"Moby-Dick" by Herman Melville was a commercial failure during the author's lifetime and gained popularity after his death.

The world's smallest book is "Teeny Ted from Turnip Town," measuring 0.07 x 0.10 millimeters.

The longest poem ever written is the "Mahabharata," an ancient Indian epic with over 1.8 million words.

"Alice's Adventures in Wonderland" by Lewis Carroll was inspired by a real-life girl named Alice Liddell.

Ernest Hemingway wrote his first novel, "The Sun Also Rises," in just six weeks.

The first printed book is the Gutenberg Bible, printed by Johannes Gutenberg in the 1450s.

The "Harry Potter" book series has been translated into over 80 languages
The term "graphic novel" was first coined by Richard Kyle in the 1960s
The world's oldest surviving poem is the "Epic of Gilgamesh," written around
2100 BCE in ancient Mesopotamia
The Braille system, used by the visually impaired, was invented by Louis
Braille when he was just 15 years old
Agatha Christie, the "Queen of Mystery," is the best-selling novelist of all
time, with over 2 billion books sold
The most expensive book ever sold was Leonardo da Vinci's notebook "Codex
Leicester," purchased by Bill Gates for over $30 million
The word "bookworm" comes from the old English word "boc-wyrm,"

referring to insects that feed on books

The "Choose Your Own Adventure" book series allows readers to make decisions and influence the story's outcome

George Orwell's "1984" and Aldous Huxley's "Brave New World" are two classic dystopian novels

The term "bestseller" was first used in the early 20th century to describe books with high sales

The world's most extensive comic book collection belongs to Robert Overstreet, with over 2 million comics

The most expensive comic book ever sold is "Action Comics #1," featuring the first appearance of Superman, sold for over $3 million

William Shakespeare's plays were first published in a collection known as the First Folio in 1623

"To Kill a Mockingbird" by Harper Lee won the Pulitzer Prize for Fiction in 1961

The term "soap opera" originated from radio dramas that were sponsored by soap companies

"Don Quixote" by Miguel de Cervantes is considered one of the first modern novels and is a classic of Western literature

The world's oldest known love poem is "Istanbul #2461," written on a clay tablet in ancient Sumeria around 2030 BCE

Roald Dahl, the author of "Charlie and the Chocolate Factory," was a fighter pilot during World War II

The "Lord of the Rings" trilogy by J.R.R. Tolkien has been adapted into highly successful film adaptations

The Guinness World Records book was first published in 1955 to settle arguments in pubs

The play "Romeo and Juliet" by William Shakespeare was first performed in
1595
Mark Twain's "Adventures of Huckleberry Finn" is considered one of the
greatest American novels
The word "nerd" was first coined by Dr. Seuss in his book "If I Ran the Zoo.
The ancient Greek epic poem "The Iliad" by Homer tells the story of the
Trojan War
Emily Dickinson, a renowned poet, wrote nearly 1,800 poems during her
lifetime but only published a few
The "Harry Potter" series has been adapted into a successful film franchise,
with eight movies released

The world's oldest surviving complete printed book is the "Diamond Sutra," printed in China in 868 CE

The "Twilight" book series by Stephenie Meyer became a cultural phenomenon and spawned a successful film series

The world's largest book is "Bhutan: A Visual Odyssey Across the Last Himalayan Kingdom," measuring 5 x 7 feet

Jane Austen's novel "Pride and Prejudice" was originally titled "First Impressions.

The term "beat generation" was coined by Jack Kerouac, author of "On the Road," to describe a group of American writers in the 1950s

3

History & Culture

The Great Wall of China is visible from space, but only under certain conditions.

The oldest known city is Jericho, dating back over 11,000 years.

The ancient Egyptian pharaoh Cleopatra was of Greek descent, not Egyptian.

The Great Pyramid of Giza was originally covered in smooth white Tura limestone casing, making it shine brightly in the sun.

The Colosseum in Rome could hold between 50,000 to 80,000 spectators and was used for various events, including gladiator fights and mock sea battles.

The first known Olympic Games were held in ancient Greece in 776 BC.

The Taj Mahal in India was built by Emperor Shah Jahan in memory of his wife Mumtaz Mahal.

The Mona Lisa was stolen from the Louvre in 1911 by an Italian handyman and was missing for over two years before being recovered.

The ancient city of Pompeii was buried under volcanic ash and preserved for centuries after the eruption of Mount Vesuvius in 79 AD.

The Gutenberg Bible, printed by Johannes Gutenberg in the 1450s, was the first major book printed using movable type in the West.

The Hanging Gardens of Babylon, one of the Seven Wonders of the Ancient World, may not have existed, according to some historical sources.

The medieval Chinese explorer Zheng He led seven epic voyages to explore the world's oceans before European exploration began.

The Eiffel Tower in Paris was originally built as a temporary structure for the 1889 World's Fair and was almost torn down afterward.

The Viking Age lasted from the late 8th century to the mid-11th century and saw Scandinavian seafarers exploring and raiding across Europe.

The Inca civilization of South America constructed the citadel of Machu Picchu in the 15th century.

The Greek philosopher Socrates never wrote any of his teachings down; everything we know about him comes from his student Plato's writings.

The city of Venice in Italy is built on a group of 118 small islands connected by canals and bridges.

The Aztec capital city of Tenochtitlan, located in present-day Mexico City, was one of the largest and most sophisticated cities in the world at its peak.

The first recorded use of the number zero as a placeholder in mathematics was in ancient India.

The Terracotta Army, a collection of thousands of life-sized statues, was buried with China's first emperor, Qin Shi Huang, to protect him in the afterlife.

The Mayan civilization of Central America developed a complex writing system using hieroglyphs.

The Rosetta Stone, discovered in Egypt in 1799, helped scholars decipher ancient Egyptian hieroglyphics.

The Han Dynasty of China (206 BC – 220 AD) is often considered one of the golden ages of Chinese history.

The 1918 influenza pandemic, also known as the Spanish flu, infected approximately one-third of the world's population and killed tens of millions of people.

The Industrial Revolution, which began in Britain in the late 18th century, transformed society by introducing mechanization and factory production.

The ancient city of Babylon was famous for its Hanging Gardens, ziggurats, and the Code of Hammurabi, one of the earliest known legal codes.

The ancient Greek philosopher Aristotle was a student of Plato and a teacher of Alexander the Great.

The first known recorded war in history is the Battle of Megiddo, which took place around 1479 BC in ancient Egypt.

The Renaissance, a period of great cultural and intellectual growth, originated in Italy during the 14th to 17th centuries.

The Seven Wonders of the Ancient World were a list of remarkable constructions in antiquity, but only the Great Pyramid of Giza still exists today.

The Berlin Wall, which divided East and West Berlin during the Cold War, fell in 1989, leading to the reunification of Germany.

The Statue of Liberty, a gift from France to the United States, was dedicated in 1886 and stands on Liberty Island in New York Harbor.

The Black Death, also known as the Bubonic Plague, was one of the deadliest pandemics in human history, killing millions of people in Europe during the 14th century.

The Sistine Chapel ceiling in Vatican City was painted by Michelangelo between 1508 and 1512 and features scenes from the Book of Genesis.

The Bronze Age, characterized by the widespread use of bronze for tools and weapons, began around 3300 BC.

The Silk Road was an ancient network of trade routes that connected Asia, Europe, and Africa for centuries.

The American Declaration of Independence was adopted on July 4, 1776, marking the United States' independence from Britain.

The Treaty of Versailles, signed in 1919, officially ended World War I and imposed heavy penalties on Germany, setting the stage for World War II.

The Battle of Waterloo in 1815 was the final defeat of Napoleon Bonaparte and marked the end of the Napoleonic Wars.
The Great Fire of London in 1666 destroyed much of the city, leading to widespread reconstruction and urban planning improvements.
The Renaissance artist Leonardo da Vinci was not only a painter but also a scientist, inventor, and anatomist.
The first known Olympic Games for women were held in Paris in 1900,

featuring events such as golf and tennis.

The first successful powered flight was achieved by the Wright brothers, Orville and Wilbur, in Kitty Hawk, North Carolina, in 1903.

The Russian Revolution in 1917 led to the establishment of the Soviet Union, which lasted until its dissolution in 1991.

The ancient Egyptian civilization lasted for over 3,000 years, making it one of the longest-lasting in history.

The Indian leader Mahatma Gandhi led the nonviolent civil disobedience movement against British rule, eventually leading to India's independence.

The Ottoman Empire, which lasted from the 13th century to 1922, was one of the most significant empires in history, spanning three continents.

The Roman Colosseum, completed in AD 80, was capable of holding 50,000 to 80,000 spectators and hosted various events, including gladiator fights and mock sea battles.

The Scottish scientist Alexander Fleming discovered penicillin by accident in 1928, revolutionizing medicine and saving countless lives.

The Siege of Troy, described in Homer's epic poem "The Iliad," is considered one of the most famous events of ancient history.

The Apollo 11 mission, launched in 1969, successfully landed astronauts Neil Armstrong and Buzz Aldrin on the moon.

The Vikings, known for their seafaring and exploration, originated from present-day Scandinavia during the Viking Age.

The ancient library of Alexandria, founded in the 3rd century BC, was one of the largest and most significant libraries of the ancient world.
The Battle of Gettysburg, fought during the American Civil War in 1863, is considered one of the bloodiest battles in U.S. history.
The Chinese philosopher Confucius (551–479 BC) is known for his teachings on ethics, morality, and social order.
The Edo period in Japan (1603–1868) was characterized by peace, stability, and the flourishing of arts and culture.
The Hundred Years' War, fought between England and France from 1337 to 1453, was a series of conflicts over territorial disputes and the English crown's claim to the French throne.

The Berlin Conference of 1884–1885 divided Africa among European powers, leading to the colonization of the continent.

The Renaissance artist Michelangelo painted the ceiling of the Sistine Chapel in Vatican City.

The fall of the Roman Empire in AD 476 marked the end of ancient Rome and the beginning of the Middle Ages.

The Black Death, also known as the Bubonic Plague, originated in Asia and spread to Europe, causing one of the most devastating pandemics in history.

The ancient city of Petra, located in present-day Jordan, was a thriving trade center and is known for its rock-cut architecture.

The Opium Wars, fought between China and Britain in the 19th century, resulted in the British gaining control over Hong Kong.

The Renaissance in Europe led to a revival of interest in classical learning, art, and culture, fostering a period of great intellectual and artistic achievement.

The English physicist Isaac Newton formulated the laws of motion and gravity, laying the foundation for classical mechanics.

The Ancient Greeks made significant contributions to philosophy, mathematics, science, and literature, influencing Western civilization.

The Neolithic Revolution, around 10,000 BC, marked the transition from hunting and gathering to agriculture, leading to settled societies and the development of civilizations.

The American Civil Rights Movement, led by figures like Martin Luther King Jr., fought for racial equality and social justice in the United States during the 1950s and 1960s.

The Great Famine in Ireland in the 1840s resulted in the death or emigration of millions of people due to potato crop failure.

The signing of the Magna Carta in 1215 by King John of England limited the monarch's power and laid the groundwork for constitutional rights.

The Crusades were a series of religious wars between Christians and Muslims over control of the Holy Land during the Middle Ages.

The Ancient Egyptians developed a sophisticated system of hieroglyphic writing, often inscribed on temple walls and monuments.

The French Revolution, beginning in 1789, led to the overthrow of the monarchy and the rise of Napoleon Bonaparte.

The Treaty of Tordesillas, signed in 1494, divided the newly discovered lands between Spain and Portugal, shaping colonial territories in the Americas.

The Louisiana Purchase, completed in 1803, doubled the size of the United States and was one of the most significant land acquisitions in history.

The Age of Exploration, spanning the 15th to 17th centuries, saw European navigators venture across the globe, opening up new trade routes and expanding geographical knowledge.

The Renaissance artist Raphael was known for his paintings and frescoes, including "The School of Athens" in the Vatican.

The abolition of slavery in the British Empire began in 1833 and was completed in 1838, leading to the emancipation of millions of enslaved people.

The Battle of Hastings in 1066 marked the Norman conquest of England, led by William the Conqueror.

The Spanish conquistador Hernán Cortés led the expedition that led to the fall of the Aztec Empire in Mexico.

The Scramble for Africa in the late 19th century saw European powers carve up and colonize much of the African continent.

The Chinese philosopher Laozi is credited with founding the philosophy of Daoism (Taoism).

The Renaissance artist Botticelli is known for his famous painting "The Birth of Venus."

The Panama Canal, completed in 1914, connects the Atlantic and Pacific

Oceans, facilitating global maritime trade.

The fall of the Byzantine Empire in 1453 marked the end of the ancient Eastern Roman Empire.

The Ancient Greeks invented the concept of democracy, where citizens participate in decision-making and governance.

The Battle of Thermopylae in 480 BC saw a small group of Spartan soldiers led by King Leonidas hold off a much larger Persian army.

The construction of the Pyramids of Egypt required an immense workforce, likely consisting of tens of thousands of laborers and skilled craftsmen.

The Industrial Revolution in Britain transformed society through mechanization, urbanization, and the rise of factories.

The Treaty of Versailles, signed in 1919, imposed severe penalties on Germany after World War I, contributing to economic hardships and political instability.

The Spanish Inquisition, established in 1478, aimed to enforce religious orthodoxy and suppress heresy, leading to widespread persecution and forced conversions.

The ancient city of Troy, famous for the Trojan War, was discovered by the German archaeologist Heinrich Schliemann in the late 19th century.

The Ottoman Empire, at its height in the 16th and 17th centuries, controlled vast territories in Europe, Asia, and Africa.

The Cold War, lasting from the mid-20th century to 1991, was a geopolitical struggle between the United States and the Soviet Union.

The Hundred Years' War between England and France, lasting from 1337 to
1453, saw significant developments in military tactics and technology.
The Berlin Wall, built in 1961 to divide East and West Berlin, became a symbol
of the Cold War's division between East and West.
The ancient city of Rome, founded in the 8th century BC, became the capital
of one of the most powerful and influential empires in history.
The Mesoamerican civilizations, including the Maya, Aztec, and Inca,
developed sophisticated systems of writing, art, and architecture.
The Second Industrial Revolution, during the late 19th and early 20th
centuries, introduced advancements in steel production, electricity, and
telecommunications.

The Russian Revolution of 1917 resulted in the overthrow of the tsarist regime and the establishment of the Soviet Union.

28

4

Nature & Animals

The Amazon Rain forest is home to approximately 10% of the known species on Earth.

Honey never spoils. Archaeologists have found edible honey in ancient Egyptian tombs over 3,000 years old.

The blue whale is the largest animal to have ever lived on Earth, with some individuals reaching over 100 feet in length.

The tongue of a blue whale can weigh as much as an elephant.

Cows have best friends and can form strong bonds with other cows.

The peacock mantis shrimp has the fastest punch in the animal kingdom, reaching speeds of over 50 miles per hour.

The pistol shrimp creates a cavitation bubble that generates heat as hot as the sun's surface when it collapses.

Sea otters hold hands while sleeping to avoid drifting apart in the water.

The chameleon's eyes can move independently, allowing them to look in two different directions simultaneously.

Venus flytraps can count to five before snapping shut and capturing their prey.

Octopuses have three hearts: two pump blood through the gills, and one pumps it through the rest of the body.

Cheetahs are the fastest land animals and can reach speeds of up to 70 miles per hour in short bursts.

Male seahorses give birth to their offspring.

The Hercules beetle can carry objects up to 850 times its body weight, making it one of the strongest creatures on Earth relative to its size.

The mimic octopus can change its shape, color, and texture to mimic other sea creatures to avoid predators.

The longest-living animal is the ocean quahog clam, which can live for more than 500 years.

Bees communicate with each other through intricate dances to indicate the location of food sources.

The star-nosed mole has 22 fleshy appendages around its nose that it uses to detect prey.

The Komodo dragon has venomous saliva, which helps to incapacitate its

prey.
A group of flamingos is called a "flamboyance."

The platypus is one of the few mammals that lay eggs.
Polar bears have black skin underneath their white fur to help absorb and retain heat from the sun.
The tongue of a giraffe can extend up to 18 inches to help them reach leaves high in trees.
The Galapagos giant tortoise can live for more than 100 years.
The axolotl is a salamander that can regenerate lost body parts, including

limbs and even parts of its brain.
The white rhinoceros is the second largest land mammal, after the elephant.
A group of crows is called a "murder."
The Archerfish can shoot a jet of water from its mouth to knock insects off overhanging leaves, making them fall into the water to eat.
The kangaroo's tail acts as a powerful fifth limb, aiding in balance and movement.
The peacock's elaborate tail feathers are used to attract females during mating displays.
Electric eels can generate electric shocks of up to 600 volts to stun prey and deter predators.
Sloths can move so slowly that algae often grow on their fur, providing camouflage in trees.
The humpback whale's song can be heard over long distances and can last up to 20 minutes.
The quokka, a small marsupial from Australia, is often referred to as the "happiest animal on Earth" due to its seemingly smiling expression.
The Siberian tiger is the largest cat species in the world, and males can weigh up to 800 pounds.
The leafcutter ant can carry leaves that are many times larger than its body back to its nest.
The axolotl remains in its larval form throughout its entire life, making it neotenic.
The Arctic fox changes its fur color to white in winter to blend with its snowy surroundings.
The bombardier beetle can spray hot, noxious chemicals from its abdomen as a defense mechanism.

The giant Pacific octopus has three hearts and blue blood.
The blue poison dart frog's skin contains a powerful neurotoxin used by indigenous people to poison their blow darts.
The horseshoe crab has been around for over 450 million years and is considered a "living fossil."
The gharial, a species of crocodile, has a long, thin snout adapted for catching fish.
The red-eyed tree frog has bright red eyes and sticks to leaves with large adhesive pads on its feet.
The African elephant is the largest land animal and can weigh up to 14,000 pounds.

The orchid mantis resembles an orchid flower and uses its appearance to ambush prey.

The ocean sunfish is the heaviest bony fish in the world, weighing up to 5,000 pounds.

The honeybee's wings beat approximately 200 times per second, enabling them to fly quickly and efficiently.

The proboscis monkey has an unusually long nose, which helps amplify its vocalizations and attract mates.

The African penguin is the only species of penguin that breeds in Africa.

5

Entertainment

The first public screening of a movie took place on December 28, 1895, by the Lumière brothers in Paris.

The Hollywood Sign originally read "Hollywoodland" and was built in 1923 as a real estate advertisement.

Walt Disney holds the record for the most Academy Awards won by an individual, with 22 Oscars.

The first television broadcast took place on September 7, 1927, by Philo Farnsworth.

The first commercial radio broadcast was on November 2, 1920, by KDKA in Pittsburgh, Pennsylvania.

"Gone with the Wind" (1939) was the first color film to win the Academy Award for Best Picture.

"Avatar" (2009) is the highest-grossing movie of all time, earning over $2.8 billion worldwide.

The longest-running Broadway show is "The Phantom of the Opera," which debuted in 1988 and is still running.

The first Grammy Awards ceremony was held in 1959.

The Beatles hold the record for the most No. 1 singles on the Billboard Hot 100 chart, with 20 songs.

Michael Jackson's "Thriller" album is the best-selling album of all time, with over 66 million copies sold.

"The Simpsons" is the longest-running scripted primetime TV series in the United States, first airing in 1989.

The video game industry's revenue surpassed the film industry's revenue in 2018.

The highest-grossing video game franchise is "Pokémon," with over $100 billion in revenue.

The first commercial video game, "Pong," was released in 1972 by Atari.

The world's first feature-length animated film is "Snow White and the Seven Dwarfs" (1937), produced by Walt Disney.

The first video ever uploaded to YouTube was titled "Me at the zoo" and was posted by co-founder Jawed Karim in 2005.

The PlayStation 2 is the best-selling video game console of all time, with over 155 million units sold.

The term "blockbuster" originally referred to a bomb powerful enough to destroy a city block, later used to describe a highly successful film.

The Academy Awards ceremony, commonly known as the Oscars, was first televised in 1953.

"Star Wars: Episode IV - A New Hope" (1977) popularized the use of special effects in the film industry.

The highest-paid actor in 2020 was Dwayne "The Rock" Johnson, earning over $87 million.

"Harry Potter and the Sorcerer's Stone" (2001) was the highest-grossing film adaptation of a book until "The Lord of the Rings: The Return of the King" (2003).

The Guinness World Records book was created by Sir Hugh Beaver in 1955 to settle bar arguments.

"The Shawshank Redemption" (1994) is often regarded as one of the greatest films of all time, despite its initial box office disappointment.

The first video game console, the Magnavox Odyssey, was released in 1972.

The first commercially successful video game was "Pong" (1972), a simplified tennis game.

The Hollywood Walk of Fame was created in 1958 and features over 2,600 stars honoring various entertainment industry professionals.

The first televised Super Bowl took place on January 15, 1967.

The first Grammy for Album of the Year was awarded to "Henry Mancini: The Music from Peter Gunn" in 1959.

The first video cassette recorder (VCR) was introduced to the public by Sony in 1963.

The Beatles' appearance on "The Ed Sullivan Show" in 1964 is considered one of the most iconic moments in television history.

The highest-grossing film franchise is the Marvel Cinematic Universe (MCU), with over $22 billion in box office revenue.

The "Star Wars" franchise has generated over $10 billion in merchandise sales since its inception.

The first video game to feature sound was "Pong Doubles" in 1973.

The first feature film ever made was "The Story of the Kelly Gang" (1906), an Australian production.

The first commercial arcade video game was "Computer Space" (1971), created by Nolan Bushnell and Ted Dabney.

The highest-grossing animated film of all time is "Frozen II" (2019), earning over $1.45 billion worldwide.

The first film with synchronized dialogue was "The Jazz Singer" (1927).

The "James Bond" film franchise is one of the longest-running in history, with over 25 films produced.

The first 3D feature film was "Bwana Devil" (1952).

The first video game character to become a cultural icon is Mario, created by Shigeru Miyamoto for Nintendo.

The Hollywood Foreign Press Association (HFPA) hosts the annual Golden

Globe Awards.

The first music video to air on MTV was "Video Killed the Radio Star" by The Buggles in 1981.

The first commercially successful video game console was the Atari 2600, released in 1977.

The first animated feature film with sound was "Snow White and the Seven Dwarfs" (1937).

The first Academy Awards ceremony was held on May 16, 1929, in Hollywood, California.

The first feature-length color film was "Becky Sharp" (1935).

The first video game to use microtransactions was "Fortnite" in 2017.

The "Harry Potter" film series is one of the highest-grossing film franchises, with over $7.7 billion in worldwide box office revenue.

6

Science

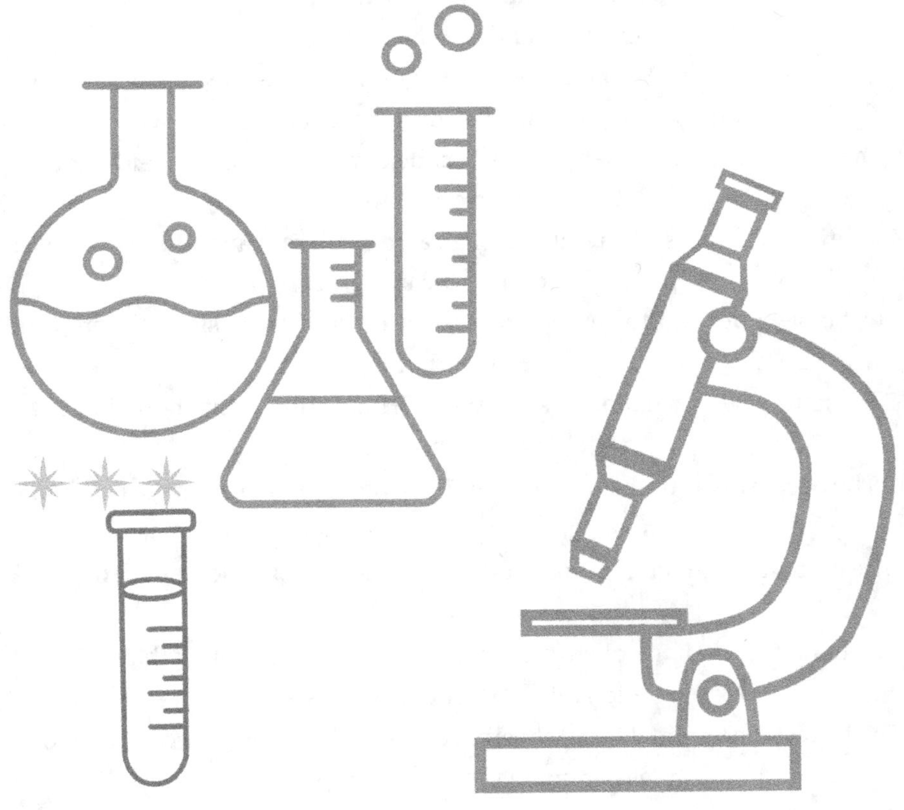

The Earth's core is hotter than the surface of the Sun.

Humans and giraffes have the same number of neck vertebrae (seven).

The speed of light in a vacuum is approximately 299,792 kilometers per second (186,282 miles per second).

The first artificial satellite, Sputnik 1, was launched by the Soviet Union on October 4, 1957.

The human brain is the most energy-consuming organ in the body, using about 20% of the body's total energy.

The concept of the Big Bang theory suggests that the universe originated from a single point and has been expanding ever since.

The chemical element helium was first discovered in the Sun before it was found on Earth.

There are more possible iterations of a game of chess than there are atoms in the observable universe.

The "blue light" emitted by electronic devices can disrupt sleep patterns and circadian rhythms.

The shortest war in history was between Britain and Zanzibar on August 27, 1896, lasting only 38 minutes.

The deepest part of the ocean is the Mariana Trench, reaching a depth of about 36,070 feet (10,994 meters).

The human body contains about 60,000 miles (97,000 kilometers) of blood vessels.

The human DNA, if uncoiled and stretched, would reach a length of about 10 billion miles (16 billion kilometers).

The fastest land animal is the cheetah, capable of reaching speeds of up to 70 miles per hour (113 kilometers per hour).

The Earth's magnetic field is what protects the planet from harmful cosmic radiation and solar winds.

The coldest temperature ever recorded on Earth was -128.6°F (-89.2°C) at the Soviet Union's Vostok Station in Antarctica in 1983.

The average human body carries about 0.2 milligrams of gold, mostly in the blood.

The Milky Way galaxy contains an estimated 100 to 400 billion stars.

The longest-living animal on record is the ocean quahog clam, which lived to be 507 years old.

The moon is gradually moving away from the Earth at a rate of about 1.5 inches (3.8 centimeters) per year.

There are more possible iterations of a game of chess than there are atoms in the observable universe.

The DNA in every human cell is damaged about 10,000 times per day but is efficiently repaired by the body's repair mechanisms.

The first successful cloning of a mammal was Dolly the sheep in 1996.

The highest temperature ever recorded on Earth was 134°F (56.7°C) in Furnace Creek, California, USA, in 1913.

The Great Barrier Reef in Australia is the largest living structure on Earth, visible from space.

The first human heart transplant was performed by Dr. Christiaan Barnard in South Africa in 1967.

The Great Red Spot on Jupiter is a massive storm that has been raging for at least 350 years.

The Sun is so large that approximately 1.3 million Earths could fit inside it.

There are about 8.7 million species of organisms on Earth, but this number could be significantly higher due to undiscovered species.

The human eye can distinguish about 10 million different colors.

The Hubble Space Telescope can capture images up to 10 billion light-years away, allowing us to see back in time.

The highest point on Earth is Mount Everest, with a peak at 29,029 feet (8,848 meters) above sea level.

Honeybees use a complex "waggle dance" to communicate the location of food sources to other members of the hive.

The Antarctic ice sheet contains about 70% of the world's freshwater.

The first successful vaccine, developed by Edward Jenner, was for smallpox in 1796.

There are about 100 billion neurons in the human brain, each forming thousands of connections with other neurons.

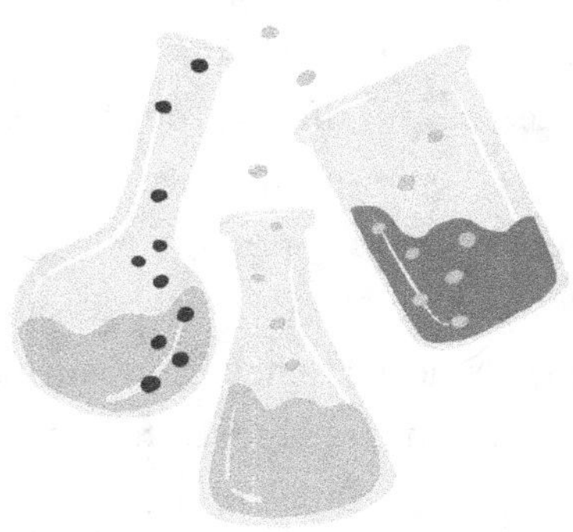

The human body is made up of about 60% water.
The element helium was first discovered on the Sun before it was found on Earth.
The ozone layer in the Earth's atmosphere absorbs most of the Sun's harmful ultraviolet radiation.
The largest volcano on Earth is Mauna Loa in Hawaii, measuring over 30,000 feet (9,144 meters) from the ocean floor to its summit.
The International Space Station (ISS) travels at a speed of approximately 17,500 miles per hour (28,000 kilometers per hour) and orbits the Earth about every 90 minutes.
The first successful heart transplant was performed in 1967 by Dr. Christiaan

Barnard in South Africa.

The Earth's core is primarily composed of iron and nickel.

The largest known dinosaur is Argentinosaurus, which may have reached lengths of up to 100 feet (30 meters) and weighed over 100 tons.

The first human to walk on the Moon was Neil Armstrong on July 20, 1969, during the Apollo 11 mission.

The DNA molecule, responsible for storing genetic information, has a double helix structure.

The element oxygen, necessary for life, is produced mainly by plants through photosynthesis.

The speed of light in a vacuum is approximately 299,792 kilometers per second (186,282 miles per second).

Jupiter's moon Europa is believed to have a subsurface ocean, making it a potential candidate for extraterrestrial life.

The human brain has a storage capacity equivalent to about 2.5 million gigabytes (or 2.5 exabytes) of digital memory.

7

Food & Drinks

Chocolate was once used as currency by the Aztecs.

Honey is the only food that does not spoil; jars of honey have been found in ancient Egyptian tombs that are over 3,000 years old and still perfectly edible.

The world's most expensive coffee is called Kopi Luwak, made from coffee beans that have been eaten and excreted by civets (small mammals).

The most widely eaten meat in the world is pork.

The world's most popular fruit is the banana.

The hottest chili pepper in the world is the Carolina Reaper, with an average Scoville rating of over 1.6 million units.

The ice cream cone was invented during the 1904 World's Fair in St. Louis when an ice cream vendor ran out of dishes and asked a nearby waffle vendor to roll up his waffles to hold the ice cream.

Carrots were originally purple; the orange color was bred into them in the 17th century by Dutch farmers to honor the royal family.

The world's largest food item is a pumpkin that weighed 2,624.6 pounds (1,190.5 kilograms).

Ketchup was originally sold as medicine in the 1830s to treat ailments like diarrhea and indigestion.

The most expensive spice in the world is saffron, derived from the stigma of the Crocus flower.

The world's oldest known recipe is for beer, dating back to ancient Sumeria around 3,900 BCE.

The longest noodle ever made measured 10,119 feet (3,085 meters) and was achieved in China.

There are over 7,500 different varieties of apples grown worldwide.

The world record for the most hamburgers eaten in three minutes is 12.
The world record for the largest pizza ever made was over 13,580 square feet (1,260 square meters) and was baked in Rome, Italy.
The hottest part of a chili pepper is the placenta, the white part that holds the seeds.
The world's largest omelet was made with 160,000 eggs in Yokohama, Japan.
Coca-Cola was originally green.
The most expensive pizza in the world costs $12,000 and is topped with edible gold, caviar, and lobster.
The word "toast" for a drinking custom comes from the ancient practice of dropping a piece of toasted bread into wine to improve its flavor.

The largest hamburger ever made weighed 2,014 pounds (913 kilograms) and was cooked in Michigan, USA.

The world record for the most hot dogs eaten in 10 minutes is 75.

Pineapples were named for their resemblance to pinecones.

In Japan, it is considered impolite to pour your own drink during a meal; instead, it is customary for others to pour it for you.

The world's largest gingerbread house covered an area of 2,520 square feet (234 square meters) and was constructed with 7,200 pounds (3,265 kilograms) of gingerbread dough.

The largest scoop of ice cream weighed 3,010 pounds (1,363 kilograms) and was created in California, USA.

Bananas are berries, but strawberries are not.

The world's oldest known winery was discovered in Armenia and dates back to around 4,100 BCE.

The first product to have a barcode was Wrigley's gum.

The world's largest cupcake weighed 1,176 pounds (533 kilograms) and was created in Washington, USA.

In ancient Rome, a "salad" was a mixture of raw vegetables seasoned with salt, vinegar, and oil.

The world's largest sushi roll measured 8,273 feet (2,522 meters) long and was created in Germany.

Peanuts are not nuts; they are legumes related to beans and lentils.

The world's largest watermelon weighed 350.5 pounds (158.8 kilograms).

The most expensive coffee in the world is made from beans that have been eaten and excreted by civets, then collected from their feces and cleaned.
The world's largest chocolate bar weighed 12,770 pounds (5,792 kilograms) and was created in the UK.
In Italy, it is considered bad luck to cut pasta before cooking it.

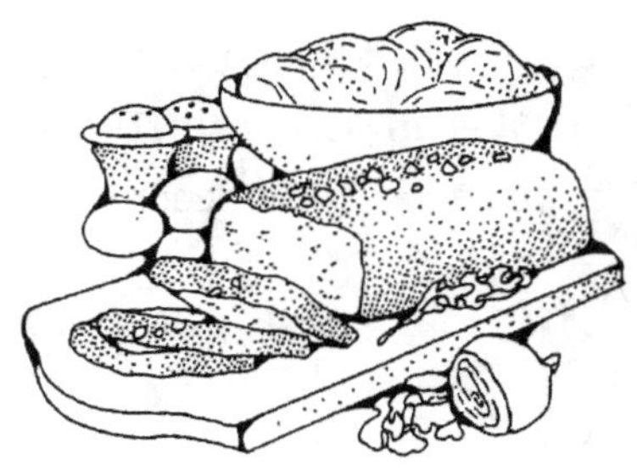

The world record for the most pancakes made in eight hours is 76,382.
The world's most expensive tequila costs over $3.5 million and is stored in a diamond-encrusted bottle.
The world's largest popcorn ball weighed 5,000 pounds (2,268 kilograms)

and was created in Ohio, USA.

The first known recipe for a sandwich dates back to the 1st century BCE in ancient Hillel, Jerusalem.

Honeybees must visit about two million flowers to produce one pound of honey.

The world's largest cake weighed 128,238 pounds (58,150 kilograms) and was made in Florida, USA.

The world record for the most jellies eaten with chopsticks in three minutes is 927.

The world's largest chocolate coin weighed 8,224 pounds (3,731 kilograms) and was created in Belgium.

The world record for the most hamburgers eaten in one minute is four.

The world's largest meatball weighed 1,110 pounds (503 kilograms) and was made in Ohio, USA.

The world's largest lollipop weighed 7,003 pounds (3,177 kilograms) and was created in Wisconsin, USA.

The world record for the most ice cream scoops balanced on a cone is 121.

8

Crime, Drugs & Prison

Crime

In the United States, the FBI's Uniform Crime Reporting Program categorizes crimes into Part I (violent crimes) and Part II (property crimes).
The term "serial killer" refers to an individual who commits multiple murders over an extended period, with a cooling-off period between each killing.
Shoplifting is one of the most common crimes globally, with millions of incidents reported each year.
The first modern fingerprint identification was performed by Sir William Herschel in British-controlled India in the 19th century.
White-collar crimes, such as fraud and embezzlement, typically involve

non-violent offenses committed by individuals in positions of trust or authority.

Cybercrime encompasses a wide range of criminal activities conducted over the internet, such as hacking, identity theft, and phishing.
Organized crime groups engage in illegal activities like drug trafficking, money laundering, and human trafficking on a large scale.
The use of forensic evidence, such as DNA analysis and fingerprinting, has revolutionized criminal investigations and helped solve many cold cases.
The United States has the highest incarceration rate in the world, with over 2

million individuals in prison or jail.

Criminal profiling is a technique used by law enforcement to create a psychological and behavioral profile of an unknown criminal based on crime scene evidence.

The theft of artwork and cultural artifacts is a significant crime, often tied to the black market for stolen goods.

The illicit trade of counterfeit goods, including counterfeit currency and luxury items, generates billions of dollars in criminal profits annually.

Identity theft occurs when someone steals personal information to commit fraud or other crimes in the victim's name.

The term "recidivism" refers to the tendency of convicted criminals to re-offend after being released from prison.

Arson is the act of deliberately setting fire to property, often to commit insurance fraud or destroy evidence.

The term "grand theft auto" originated from the crime of stealing an automobile and is often associated with carjacking and vehicle theft.

Kidnapping is the unlawful abduction and restraint of a person against their will, often involving demands for ransom.

Hate crimes involve criminal acts motivated by prejudice or bias against a particular race, religion, gender, or other characteristics.

The "CSI effect" refers to the influence of crime dramas on public perception and expectations of forensic evidence in real criminal cases.

The death penalty is still practiced in several countries, with lethal injection being the most common method of execution.

Drugs

The United Nations Office on Drugs and Crime estimates that around 275 million people worldwide used drugs at least once in 2020.

The use of psychoactive substances dates back thousands of years, with evidence of drug use found in ancient civilizations.

The term "controlled substances" refers to drugs that are regulated by law due to their potential for abuse and addiction.

The opioid crisis, particularly in the United States, has led to a surge in opioid-related deaths and addiction.
The recreational use of cannabis (marijuana) is now legal in several countries and states, but it remains illegal in many places.
MDMA (ecstasy) was originally developed as a pharmaceutical drug to assist in psychotherapy but became popular as a recreational drug.
Cocaine is derived from the coca plant and is known for its stimulant effects.
Prescription drug abuse is a growing problem, with many people misusing medications obtained legally through prescriptions.
Heroin is an opioid drug made from morphine, and its use is associated with a high risk of overdose and addiction.
Drug trafficking is a significant criminal enterprise, with illegal drug trade networks operating globally.
Alcohol is the most widely used psychoactive substance in the world.
Methamphetamine is a powerful stimulant drug associated with severe health consequences and addiction.
LSD (lysergic acid diethylamide) is a hallucinogenic drug known for its mind-altering effects.

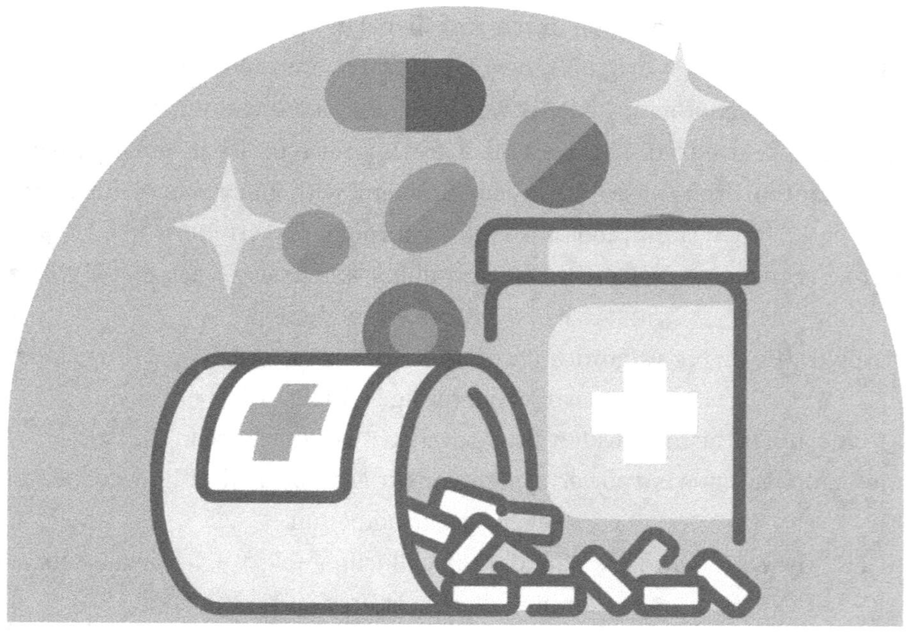

"Club drugs" are substances often associated with dance clubs and parties, including MDMA, GHB, and ketamine.

"Date rape drugs," such as Rohypnol and GHB, are used to facilitate sexual assault by rendering victims unconscious or disoriented.

The "war on drugs" is a term used to describe global efforts to combat drug trafficking and abuse.

Drug abuse can lead to various health issues, including liver damage, heart problems, and mental health disorders.

Prescription opioids are often diverted for non-medical use, contributing to the opioid epidemic.

The use of performance-enhancing drugs (doping) is a significant issue in professional sports.

Substance use disorders are recognized as medical conditions, and treatment options are available to help individuals recover from addiction.

Prison

The concept of incarceration as a form of punishment dates back to ancient civilizations like ancient Greece and Rome.

The United States has the highest number of incarcerated individuals per capita, with overcrowding being a significant issue in many prisons.

"Supermax" prisons are high-security facilities designed to house the most dangerous and violent criminals.

The prison system aims to serve several purposes, including punishment, rehabilitation, and deterrence.

Solitary confinement, also known as "the hole" or "the box," involves isolating prisoners in small cells for extended periods, which can have severe psychological effects.

Prison labor is used in many countries, with inmates performing various tasks and jobs within the prison system.

The "three strikes" law in some countries imposes harsher penalties for individuals convicted of multiple serious offenses.

The process of releasing a prisoner before the completion of their full sentence is known as parole.

"Prison overcrowding" occurs when the number of inmates exceeds the capacity of a facility, leading to a variety of issues, including violence and reduced access to resources.

The practice of imprisoning individuals for minor, non-violent offenses has led to debates about the effectiveness and fairness of the criminal justice system.

64

9

Human Body & Human Behavior

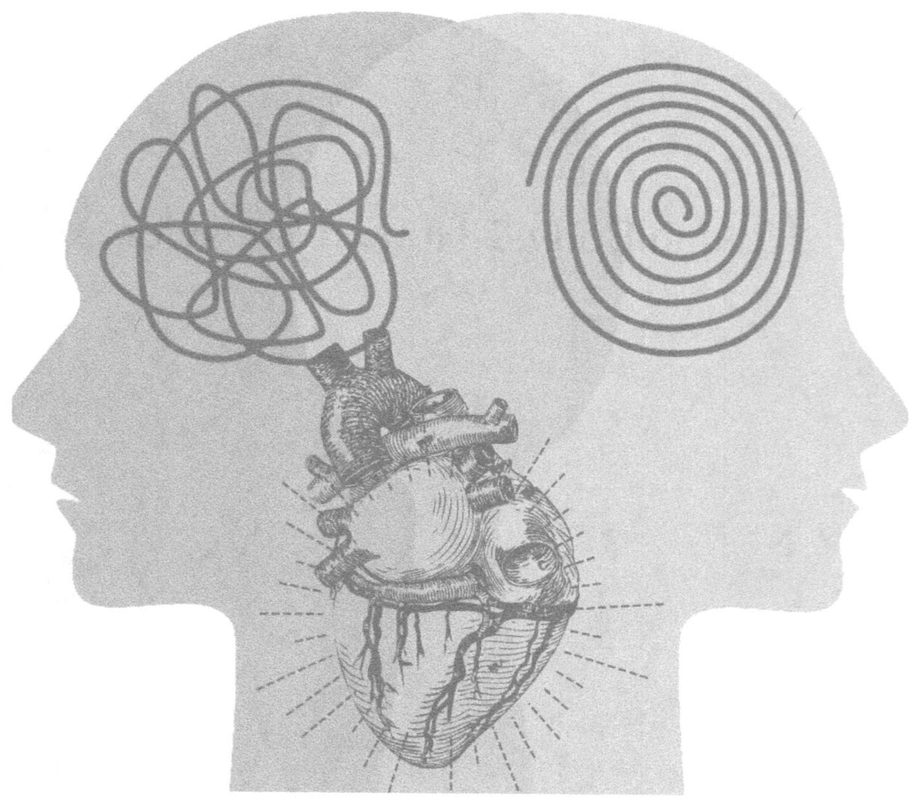

Human Body

The human body contains approximately 206 bones.
The smallest bone in the human body is the stapes bone in the ear.
The human brain weighs about 3 pounds (1.4 kilograms) on average.
The liver is the largest internal organ in the human body.
The human heart pumps about 2,000 gallons (7,571 liters) of blood daily.
Human taste buds are replaced approximately every two weeks.
The average human has about 100,000 hairs on their scalp.
The human body contains enough carbon to make about 9,000 pencils.
The human body contains enough iron to make a small nail.

Sneezes can travel at speeds of up to 100 miles per hour (161 kilometers per hour).

Human beings are the only mammals that cry emotional tears.

The average person produces about 25,000 quarts (23,658 liters) of saliva in their lifetime.

The length of all the blood vessels in the human body, if stretched end to end, would circle the Earth over twice.

The human eye can distinguish approximately 10 million different colors.

The human body has over 600 individual skeletal muscles.

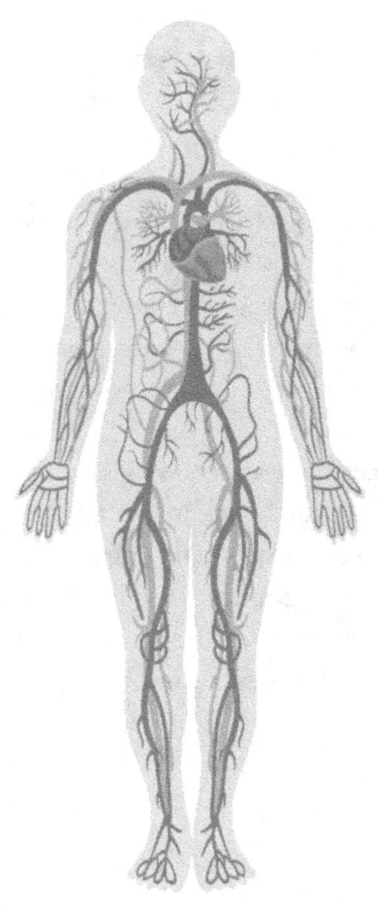

The human nose can detect over 1 trillion different scents.
The strongest muscle in the human body is the masseter, responsible for chewing.
Humans are born with 300 bones, but some fuse together as we grow, resulting in the adult total of 206.
The human eye blinks about 15-20 times per minute on average.
The surface area of the human lungs is roughly the size of a tennis court.

Human Behavior

Yawning is contagious and can trigger a similar response in others.
People tend to be more attracted to others who have similar facial features to their own.
The "bystander effect" is a phenomenon where individuals are less likely to help in an emergency when others are present.
The "placebo effect" refers to the beneficial effects experienced by some individuals who receive a placebo (inactive substance) believing it to be a real treatment.
Body language is an essential aspect of communication, with nonverbal cues often conveying more than verbal language.
The human brain can recognize and process a familiar face in less than a second.
The "Pygmalion effect" describes how higher expectations placed upon individuals can lead to improved performance.
Humans are wired to feel empathy, and mirror neurons in the brain play a role in understanding and mirroring the emotions of others.
"Confirmation bias" is the tendency to seek, interpret, and favor information that confirms preexisting beliefs or opinions.

The "mere exposure effect" suggests that people tend to develop a preference for things simply because they are familiar with them.
The "fight or flight" response is a physiological reaction to stress that prepares the body to confront or flee from a threat.
Human memory is susceptible to distortion, and false memories can be implanted through suggestion or misinformation.
The "Hawthorne effect" refers to the phenomenon of individuals modifying their behavior when they know they are being observed.
The "halo effect" is a cognitive bias where a positive impression of a person in one area leads to an overall positive evaluation of that person.
Humans tend to perceive faces in random patterns or objects—a

phenomenon known as "pareidolia."

The "self-serving bias" is the tendency to attribute successes to internal factors and failures to external factors.

People tend to remember incomplete or interrupted tasks more than completed ones due to the Zeigarnik effect.

"Deja vu" is a phenomenon where a person feels that they have experienced a situation before, even though it is the first time.

The "chameleon effect" is an unconscious tendency to mimic the behavior, mannerisms, or expressions of others during social interactions.

Human behavior is influenced by both nature (genetics) and nurture (environmental factors).

The "Dunning-Kruger effect" is a cognitive bias where people with low ability in a particular area overestimate their competence.

The "recency effect" is the tendency to remember information encountered most recently better than information encountered earlier.

The "primacy effect" is the tendency to remember information encountered first better than information encountered later.

The "stereotype threat" is the phenomenon where individuals experience anxiety or reduced performance due to the fear of confirming negative stereotypes about their social group.

The "fundamental attribution error" is the tendency to attribute other people's behavior to internal characteristics rather than external circumstances.

The "Oedipus complex" is a psychoanalytic theory that suggests boys have unconscious feelings of desire for their mothers and jealousy of their fathers.

The "Milgram experiment" revealed people's willingness to obey authority figures, even if it resulted in harm to others.

The "Asch conformity experiments" demonstrated the influence of group pressure on individual decision-making and perception.

The "Pavlovian response" is a form of classical conditioning where a neutral stimulus becomes associated with a reflexive response.

Human behavior is shaped by a combination of genetics, environment, culture, and individual experiences.

10

Bizarre

A group of flamingos is called a "flamboyance."
There are more possible iterations of a game of chess than there are atoms in the observable universe.
The shortest war in history was between Britain and Zanzibar on August 27, 1896, lasting only 38 minutes.
The "recency illusion" is a cognitive bias where people believe that things are more recent than they actually are.
Scotland's national animal is the unicorn.
A day on Venus is longer than a year on Venus. It takes Venus about 243 Earth days to rotate on its axis and only about 225 Earth days to orbit the Sun.
The inventor of the frisbee was turned into a frisbee after he died when he

requested to be cremated and turned into a toy.

The longest wedding veil was longer than 1.8 miles (2.9 kilometers).

A group of crows is called a "murder."

"Hippopotomonstrosesquippedaliophobia" is the fear of long words.

Honey never spoils; archaeologists have found pots of honey in ancient Egyptian tombs that are over 3,000 years old and still perfectly edible.

The electric chair was invented by a dentist.

Wombat feces are cube-shaped.

In 1998, Sony accidentally sold 700,000 camcorders that had the technology to see through people's clothes.

Octopuses have three hearts.

A group of owls is called a "parliament."

The shortest verse in the Bible is John 11:35, "Jesus wept."

The Hawaiian alphabet only has 12 letters: A, E, H, I, K, L, M, N, O, P, U, and W.

A cat has 32 muscles in each ear.

The oldest "yo mama" joke dates back to 1500 BCE.

There is a restaurant in Tokyo, Japan, that serves food in toilets.

The oldest known piece of chewing gum is over 9,000 years old.

The longest time between two twins being born is 87 days.

The Eiffel Tower can be 15 centimeters taller during the summer due to thermal expansion.

Humans and giraffes have the same number of neck vertebrae (seven).

A "butt" was a medieval unit of measurement for wine, equal to 126 gallons.

The smell of freshly cut grass is a plant distress call, produced when the grass is injured.

Some birds can sleep while flying, a phenomenon known as "unihemispheric slow-wave sleep."

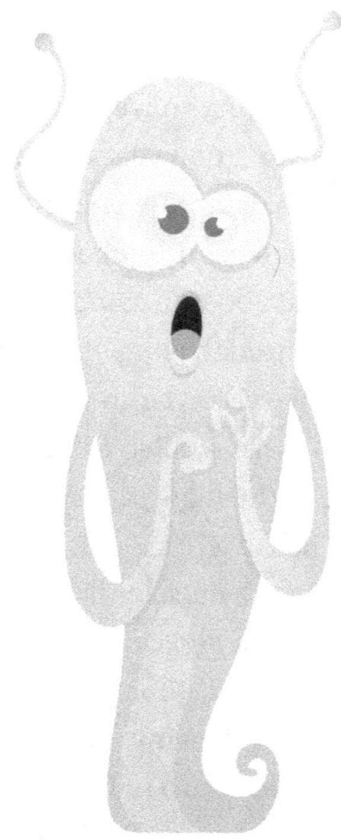

The world's oldest known living tree is estimated to be around 5,000 years old.

A "jiffy" is an actual unit of time, defined as 1/100th of a second.

A group of pugs is called a "grumble."

The surface area of Russia is larger than the surface area of Pluto.

The human body contains enough carbon to make about 9,000 pencils.

The world record for the longest time between twins being born is 87 days.

The "Avocado Hand" is a term used to describe the injuries people get while trying to remove the pit from an avocado.

In 1518, there was a "dancing plague" in Strasbourg, France, where hundreds of people danced uncontrollably for days.

There is a basketball court on the top floor of the U.S. Supreme Court building.

The dot over the letter "i" is called a "tittle."

A group of ferrets is called a "business."

Maine is the only U.S. state with a one-syllable name.

The tongue is the strongest muscle in the human body relative to its size.

The electric chair was invented by a dentist.

Coca-Cola was originally green.

A group of hedgehogs is called an "array."

Bananas are berries, but strawberries are not.

The world's longest sausage measured 36.75 miles (59.2 kilometers).

The "Buffalo buffalo Buffalo buffalo buffalo buffalo Buffalo buffalo" sentence is grammatically correct.

The "recency illusion" is a cognitive bias where people believe that things are more recent than they actually are.

The first man-made object to break the sound barrier was a whip.

The Bible is the most shoplifted book in the world.

11

Sports

Basketball was invented in 1891 by Dr. James Naismith.
Golf is the only sport to have been played on the moon; astronaut Alan Shepard hit a golf ball during the Apollo 14 mission in 1971.
Table tennis balls were once made of celluloid, but they are now made of plastic.
The first modern Olympic Games were held in Athens, Greece, in 1896.
The first game of American football was played between Rutgers and Princeton on November 6, 1869.
The first Wimbledon tennis championship took place in 1877.
Cricket is the second most popular sport in the world, with over 2.5 billion fans.

The first World Series in baseball was held in 1903 between the Boston Red Sox and the Pittsburgh Pirates.

The fastest recorded tennis serve was 163.4 mph (263.4 km/h) by Sam Groth of Australia in 2012.

Michael Jordan, widely regarded as one of the greatest basketball players of all time, won six NBA championships with the Chicago Bulls.

The record for the highest individual score in a Test cricket match is 400 runs by Brian Lara of the West Indies.

The fastest ever recorded pitch in baseball was 105.1 mph (169.1 km/h) thrown by Aroldis Chapman in 2010.

The longest recorded baseball game lasted 33 innings and was played between the Pawtucket Red Sox and the Rochester Red Wings in 1981.

The first modern Olympic champion was James Connolly of the United States, who won the triple jump event in 1896.

The Super Bowl is the most-watched sporting event in the United States, with over 100 million viewers annually.

Usain Bolt of Jamaica holds the world record for the 100-meter sprint with a time of 9.58 seconds, set in 2009.

The highest-scoring football match in history was a 149-0 victory for AS Adema against Stade Olympique de l'Emyrne in Madagascar in 2002. Adema scored 149 own goals as a protest.

The longest recorded field goal in NFL history was 64 yards, kicked by Matt Prater in 2013.

The first recorded game of baseball was played in 1846 in Hoboken, New Jersey.

The most successful country in the history of the Summer Olympics is the United States, with over 1,000 gold medals.

The most successful country in the history of the Winter Olympics is Norway, with over 130 gold medals.

The oldest continuous trophy in sports is the America's Cup, first awarded in 1851.

Cricket is the national sport of England and has been played there since the 16th century.

The world record for the longest home run in baseball is 582 feet (177.4 meters) hit by Mickey Mantle in 1953.
The oldest football club in the world is Sheffield FC, founded in England in 1857.
The Tour de France, one of the most famous cycling races, was first held in 1903.
The record for the most points scored in an NBA basketball game is 100, set by Wilt Chamberlain in 1962.
The first modern Olympic gold medal was won by American James B. Connolly in the triple jump event in 1896.
The oldest surviving football trophy is the Youdan Cup, first contested in 1867.

The first recorded game of golf was played in Scotland in 1457.

Michael Phelps, an American swimmer, holds the record for the most Olympic gold medals, with 23.

The fastest goal scored in a soccer World Cup was by Hakan Şükür of Turkey, who scored in 11 seconds in 2002.

The first baseball game to be broadcast on radio was between the Pirates and the Phillies in 1921.

The longest recorded tennis match lasted 11 hours and 5 minutes, played between John Isner and Nicolas Mahut at Wimbledon in 2010.

The first-ever FIFA World Cup was held in 1930 in Uruguay, and the host country won the tournament.

The Stanley Cup, awarded to the winner of the NHL playoffs, was first awarded in 1893.

The first recorded soccer match was played in 1863 between two teams of London clubs under the new Football Association rules.

The fastest goal ever scored in soccer was in 2.8 seconds by Nawaf Al Abed of Saudi Arabia in 2009.

The first modern Olympic Games did not include women's events; women first competed in the 1900 Paris Olympics.

The first game of modern basketball was played with a soccer ball and two peach baskets.

The Boston Celtics hold the record for the most NBA championships, with 17 titles.

The first recorded game of rugby was played in 1823 when William Webb Ellis picked up the ball and ran with it during a soccer match at Rugby School in England.

The record for the most points scored in a single NBA game is 100, set by Wilt Chamberlain in 1962.

The first official international soccer match was played between England and Scotland in 1872.

The highest-scoring basketball game in NBA history was a 186-184 victory for the Detroit Pistons over the Denver Nuggets in 1983.

The first recorded game of tennis was played in France in the 12th century.

The first modern Olympic Games had only male participants; the first female Olympians competed in 1900.

The first recorded game of ice hockey was played in 1875 in Montreal, Canada.

The first World Series was held in 1903 between the Boston Red Sox and the Pittsburgh Pirates.

The first official cricket test match was played between England and Australia in 1877.

12

Technology & Inventions

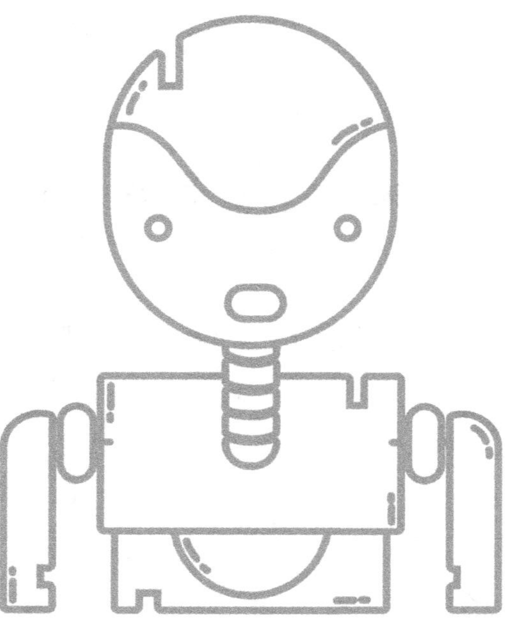

The first computer programmer was Ada Lovelace, who wrote the first
algorithm for Charles Babbage's analytical engine in the mid-1800s.
The first email was sent in 1971 by Ray Tomlinson, who used the "@" symbol
to designate the destination address.
The World Wide Web was invented by Sir Tim Berners-Lee in 1989.
The first mobile phone call was made in 1973 by Martin Cooper, a Motorola
engineer, using a prototype handheld phone.
The computer mouse was invented by Douglas Engelbart in 1964.
The first commercial video game was "Pong," released in 1972 by Atari.
The barcode was invented by Norman Joseph Woodland and Bernard Silver in
the late 1940s.

The first functional smartphone was IBM's Simon Personal Communicator, released in 1994.

The first public demonstration of a television was made by John Logie Baird in 1925.

The first commercially successful personal computer was the Altair 8800, introduced in 1975.

The first website, info.cern.ch, was launched by Tim Berners-Lee in 1991.

The first camera phone was the Kyocera Visual Phone VP-210, released in Japan in 1999.

The first commercial GPS satellite was launched in 1978.

The first 1GB hard drive was released by IBM in 1980, and it weighed over 500 pounds.

The first commercial digital camera was the Fuji DS-1P, released in 1988.

The first successful flight of the Wright brothers' airplane was on December 17, 1903.

The first mass-produced automobile was the Model T, introduced by Henry Ford in 1908.

The first practical incandescent light bulb was invented by Thomas Edison in 1879.

The first touchscreen smartphone was IBM's Simon Personal Communicator, released in 1994.

The first commercial video cassette recorder (VCR) was introduced by Sony in 1971.

The first commercial electric dishwasher was introduced in 1913.

The first portable music player, the Sony Walkman, was introduced in 1979.

The first color television was introduced by RCA in 1954.

The first successful transatlantic telegraph cable was completed in 1866.

The first computer hard disk drive was the IBM 350 Disk File, introduced in 1956.

The first modern computer, ENIAC, was completed in 1945 and weighed over

27 tons.

The first computer mouse was made of wood and had only one button.

The first computer with a graphical user interface (GUI) was the Xerox Alto, developed in the 1970s.

The first successful telephone call was made by Alexander Graham Bell in 1876 to his assistant, Thomas Watson.

The first compact disc (CD) was produced by Sony and Philips in 1982.

The first commercial laser printer was introduced by IBM in 1975.

The first portable cell phone was the Motorola DynaTAC 8000X, released in 1983.

The first commercial microwave oven was introduced in 1947.

The first successful flight of a powered airplane was made by the Wright brothers on December 17, 1903.

The first website domain, symbolics.com, was registered on March 15, 1985.

The first practical telephone was invented by Alexander Graham Bell in 1876.

The first integrated circuit (microchip) was invented by Jack Kilby in 1958.

The first electric light bulb was invented by Sir Joseph Swan in 1878, a year before Thomas Edison's version.

The first computer with a mouse-driven graphical user interface (GUI) was the Apple Lisa, introduced in 1983.

The first public demonstration of the television was made by Philo Farnsworth in 1927.

The first successful flight of a powered, controlled, and sustained airplane was made by the Wright brothers on December 17, 1903.

The first electric washing machine was patented in 1908.
The first modern digital computer, the Electronic Numerical Integrator and Computer (ENIAC), was completed in 1945.
The first computer hard disk drive, the IBM 350 Disk File, was introduced in 1956 and had a capacity of 5 megabytes.
The first digital camera was developed by Steven Sasson at Kodak in 1975, and it weighed 8 pounds.
The first practical sewing machine was invented by Elias Howe in 1846.
The first successful test of the first practical telephone was made by Alexander Graham Bell in 1876.
The first commercial video game console, the Magnavox Odyssey, was

released in 1972.

The first commercial electric refrigerator was introduced in 1913.

The first successful airplane was flown by the Wright brothers in 1903.

13

Languages

There are over 7,000 languages spoken in the world today.
The most widely spoken language in the world is Mandarin Chinese, followed by Spanish and English.
Papua New Guinea has the most languages spoken within its borders, with over 800 languages.
The language with the most native speakers is Mandarin Chinese, spoken by over a billion people.
The longest word in the English language is "pneumonoultramicroscopicsilicovolcanoconiosis."
The shortest complete sentence in the English language is "I am."
The oldest written language still in use is believed to be Sumerian, dating back

to around 3200 BCE.

The Bible has been translated into more than 3,000 languages, making it the most translated book in the world.

The word "alphabet" comes from the first two letters of the Greek alphabet: alpha and beta.

The most difficult language to learn for English speakers is considered to be Mandarin Chinese, followed by Arabic and Korean.

The most common vowel sound in the world's languages is the "a" sound, as in "father."

The first known alphabet, developed by the Phoenicians, consisted of 22 letters.

The word "hello" is one of the most universally recognized words in the world.

The English language has borrowed words from over 350 different languages.

The word "grammar" comes from the Greek word "grammatikē," which means "art of letters."

There is a language in Mexico called "Chinantec," which has the most complex tonal system in the world.

The most translated book in the world after the Bible is "The Little Prince" by Antoine de Saint-Exupéry.

The sentence "The quick brown fox jumps over the lazy dog" contains every letter of the English alphabet.

The Russian language uses the Cyrillic alphabet, which was developed in the 9th century by Saint Cyril.

The Basque language, spoken in Spain and France, is considered a language isolate, meaning it has no known relation to any other language.

The Welsh language has more vowels than the English language.

The word "computer" used to refer to a person who performed calculations manually, not a machine.

The word "bookkeeper" and "bookkeeping" are the only unhyphenated English words with three consecutive double letters.

In Japanese, there are three writing systems: hiragana, katakana, and kanji.
The word "alphabetical" is the longest word in the English language with all
its letters in alphabetical order.
Approximately one in four people in the world speak some level of English.
The Hawaiian language has only 13 letters in its alphabet.
"E" is the most commonly used letter in the English language.
The language with the most consonants in its alphabet is Ubykh, a
now-extinct language from the Caucasus region.
The word "book" is one of the oldest words in the English language, dating
back over 1,000 years.
The Finnish language has no gendered pronouns.

The Cherokee syllabary, developed by Sequoyah in the early 19th century, is one of the few writing systems created by a single person.
The term "onomatopoeia" refers to words that imitate the sound they represent, such as "buzz" or "moo."
The word "language" comes from the Latin word "lingua," which means "tongue."
The word "goodbye" is a contraction of "God be with you."
The word "time" is the most commonly used noun in English.
The indigenous language of whistling, Silbo Gomero, is still used in the Canary Islands to communicate across long distances.
The word "serendipity" was coined by Horace Walpole in 1754 based on a Persian fairy tale titled "The Three Princes of Serendip."

Hebrew was a dead language for centuries but was revived as the official language of Israel in 1948.

The word "ampersand" is a contraction of "and per se and," meaning "and by itself."

The word "oxymoron" is itself an example of an oxymoron, as it combines "oxys" (sharp) and "moros" (dull).

The first known written inscription in the Chinese language dates back to the Shang Dynasty (c. 1500–1046 BCE).

The letter "A" is the only letter that appears in the written form of every number (e.g., one, two, three).

The word "set" has the most definitions of any word in the English language.

The Hawaiian alphabet contains only 12 letters: A, E, I, O, U, H, K, L, M, N, P, and W.

The Korean alphabet, called Hangul, was created in the 15th century to increase literacy among the common people.

The word "phonetics" comes from the Greek word "phōne," which means "sound" or "voice."

The word "unfriend" was added to the Oxford English Dictionary in 2009.

The letter "E" appears in more than 11% of all English words.

The oldest written records of the English language are runic inscriptions from the 5th century.

14

Books & Comic books

The world's largest library is the Library of Congress in the United States, which houses over 170 million items.

The Gutenberg Bible, printed in 1455, was the first major book printed using movable metal type in Europe.

"Don Quixote" by Miguel de Cervantes is considered the first modern novel and was published in two parts in 1605 and 1615.

The longest sentence in literature is found in "Ulysses" by James Joyce and consists of 4,391 words.

The Harry Potter book series, written by J.K. Rowling, has sold over 500 million copies worldwide, making it one of the best-selling book series of all time.

Agatha Christie is the best-selling novelist of all time, with over 2 billion copies of her books sold.

The novel "1984" by George Orwell introduced the concept of "Big Brother" and popularized the term "Orwellian."

The first novel written on a typewriter was "Tom Sawyer" by Mark Twain.

"The Lord of the Rings" by J.R.R. Tolkien has been translated into over 50 languages.

The "Harry Potter" series has been translated into 80 languages, including Latin and Ancient Greek.

The longest novel ever written is "In Search of Lost Time" by Marcel Proust, with over 1.5 million words.

"Alice's Adventures in Wonderland" by Lewis Carroll was originally written as a gift for Alice Liddell, the daughter of a family friend.

The word "bookworm" was first used in the 16th century to describe a person who loved to read.

The "Choose Your Own Adventure" series, created by Edward Packard and R.A. Montgomery, allowed readers to make choices that affected the outcome of the story.

"War and Peace" by Leo Tolstoy is one of the longest novels ever written, with over 1,200 pages in some editions.

The Bible is the best-selling book of all time, with over 5 billion copies sold.

The world's smallest book is "Teeny Ted from Turnip Town," measuring 0.07 x 0.10 millimeters.

The first novel ever written on a typewriter was "The Adventures of Tom Sawyer" by Mark Twain.

The first book printed in English was "Recuyell of the Historyes of Troye" by William Caxton, printed in 1473.

The phrase "out of the frying pan, into the fire" originated from "The Hobbit" by J.R.R. Tolkien.

"The Catcher in the Rye" by J.D. Salinger was originally intended for adults but became popular with young readers.

The first known comic book, "The Adventures of Obadiah Oldbuck," was published in 1837.

"Moby-Dick" by Herman Melville was initially a commercial failure but is now considered one of the greatest American novels.

The term "graphic novel" was popularized by Will Eisner in 1978 for his work "A Contract with God."

The "Twilight" book series by Stephenie Meyer has sold over 100 million copies worldwide.

The author J.K. Rowling wrote the "Harry Potter" series in coffee shops while struggling financially.

"To Kill a Mockingbird" by Harper Lee won the Pulitzer Prize for Fiction in 1961.

The novel "Dracula" by Bram Stoker introduced the iconic character of Count Dracula.

The "Star Wars" novel "Heir to the Empire" by Timothy Zahn is considered the first book of the Star Wars Expanded Universe.

The "Game of Thrones" book series by George R.R. Martin is titled "A Song of Ice and Fire."

The "Diary of Anne Frank" is one of the most widely read books in the world, documenting Anne's life during the Holocaust.

The first detective novel is considered to be "The Murders in the Rue Morgue" by Edgar Allan Poe.

The world's oldest surviving book is the Diamond Sutra, a Buddhist text printed in 868 CE.

The term "bestseller" was first used in the 19th century to describe books with rapid and widespread sales.

The "Goosebumps" book series by R.L. Stine has sold over 400 million copies worldwide.

"The Chronicles of Narnia" book series by C.S. Lewis has been translated into over 47 languages.

"The Wonderful Wizard of Oz" by L. Frank Baum was published in 1900 and became an instant bestseller.

The book "The Little Prince" by Antoine de Saint-Exupéry has been translated into over 300 languages.

The first printed book using movable type was "The Diamond Sutra," a Buddhist text, in 868 CE.

The term "comic book" originated from the first comic book published in 1933, titled "Famous Funnies."

"Gone with the Wind" by Margaret Mitchell won the Pulitzer Prize for Fiction in 1937.

"Pride and Prejudice" by Jane Austen was originally titled "First Impressions."

The word "book" comes from the Old English word "bōc," which means "a written document."

The "His Dark Materials" trilogy by Philip Pullman has been adapted into a

successful TV series.
The "Jack Reacher" book series by Lee Child has sold over 100 million copies worldwide.
The novel "The Great Gatsby" by F. Scott Fitzgerald is considered one of the greatest works of American literature.
"The Hunger Games" trilogy by Suzanne Collins has been adapted into a successful film series.
"The Da Vinci Code" by Dan Brown became one of the best-selling novels of the 21st century.
The "A Song of Ice and Fire" book series inspired the popular TV series "Game of Thrones."
"Pippi Longstocking" by Astrid Lindgren is one of the most translated and beloved children's books worldwide.